ASTRONOMY

An Introduction

Hermann von Baravalle

Edited and revised by Norman Davidson

RSCP

The publisher is grateful for the encouragement and support of Robert Dulaney in making this new edition possible.

ISBN 0-945803-47-8

Table of Contents

INTRODUCTION

Hermann von Baravalle was a pioneer in kindling and spreading the flame of humanness, enthusiasm, and warmth of heart in his development of mathematics and science, in an age which increasingly developed external technicality alone at the expense of such a human approach. Above all, he was a teacher—of both children and adults—and there have been many witnesses throughout the middle years of the 20th century who have attested, as students or audience, to his gifts for inspiring either scientific or non-scientific minds about the living phenomena of the earth and universe.

Born in Vienna in 1898, von Baravalle became acquainted with Rudolf Steiner's teachings during the First World War. Later he completed a doctorate in philosophy at the University of Vienna. His inaugural dissertation in 1921 already expressed his ideas on education, and was entitled "On Teaching Physics and Mathematics" (Mercury Press, Spring Valley, NY, 1993). The section on teaching astronomy prefigured, for example in its treatment of the phases of the moon, what was to appear years later in this present little book.

In 1921 he joined the faculty of Rudolf Steiner's Waldorf school in Stuttgart, teaching mathematics and physics. He stayed there for 16 years, also contributing to the Waldorf Teacher Training Seminar. Behind this educational work stood his firm commitment to Rudolf Steiner's anthroposophy as a spiritual path. In 1920, even before von Baravalle's university graduation, Steiner invited him to lecture at the as-yet unfinished first Goetheanum building in Switzerland— the anthroposophical world center.

Dr. Baravalle visited the United States in 1933, along with his fellow anthroposophical pioneers Ehrenfried Pfeiffer and Guenther

Wachsmuth. Later, in 1937, he emigrated to the USA and became an American Citizen in 1944.

During the years following his arrival in North America, Dr. Baravalle's activities flourished in a comprehensive way. He gave many lecture tours from coast to coast over a number of years on a wide variety of subjects, involving education, science and cultural questions. He was active in the founding of several Waldorf schools and was a leading figure in Waldorf Teacher Training. Living first in the eastern United States, he became Chairman of the Mathematics Department of Adelphi College in Garden City, Long Island, where a Waldorf Teacher Education Program was started under his directorship. He became Educational Consultant of a Waldorf Demonstration School of Adelphi, which later evolved into the Garden City Waldorf School.

During his time on the west coast, he was involved in the founding of a Teacher Training Program at Highland Hall Waldorf School in California, and was co-Director of the Waldorf Teacher Training Center in Los Angeles.

Dr. Baravalle became a widely-known figure in the realms of mathematics and education in general. He has appeared in the columns of, for example, *Scientific American,* and *Life* magazine—a full page of *Life* being devoted to him in photographs and text on March 21, 1949. His own articles appeared in such publications as *The Mathematics Teacher* and *Scripta Mathematica*. Dr. Baravalle himself, besides teaching and lecturing, was the author of a wide range of books and monographs in English and German.

Dr. Baravalle suffered a stroke in 1969. He entered a nursing home in Germany and died there in 1973. One year later, this present volume received its first publication and was called *Astronomy: An Introduction*, under the series title *Waldorf School Monographs*, and was produced in the USA. I am told that the manuscript had been discovered among Dr. Baravalle's belongings after his death.

The book was later reprinted in 1991 by Rudolf Steiner College Publications, under the front cover title of *Introduction to Astronomy in the Sixth Grade of the Waldorf Schools.*

The fact is that the manuscript, in the form it appeared in before now, required extensive editing. Knowing Dr. Baravalle's work and reputation, I doubt that he had a chance to edit or revise the text himself. It read like a rough draft extracted from his well-known German book on astronomy *Die Erscheinungen am Sternenhimmel.*

Besides dealing with various technical problems as best I could, I have tried to clarify, with more detail, what the author was saying, and update the text where necessary—while retaining the essence of his original style and layout. Concerning up-dating and adjustments, for example:

> The June solstice moved from the constellation of Gemini and into Taurus about a decade ago.
>
> There is the unexpected fact that Mercury, unlike Venus, is brightest when in its gibbous to full phase; that is, seen from earth, when Mercury is on its path which passes behind the sun, between greatest elongations west and east. Venus is brightest when in crescent phase and on its path which passes between sun and earth.
>
> I have added some details about the precession of the equinoxes and its effect on the dates when the sun enters particular constellations in the course of the year—its entry into Libra, for instance, is gradually sliding from October into November.

On another level, I have striven to amplify Dr. Baravalle's particular approach to apparent star paths for the observer on earth. I have tried to bring together a two-dimensional view of the turning sky with a three-dimensional one in relation to his drawings and text at the start of the book. This involves the whole question of seeing, of mental picturing, and of geometrical perspective.

It was partly through reading this book around 25 years ago that I was stimulated to take up such subtle questions involving a direct, personal encounter with nature's phenomena, and begin research into an experience-based and humanly-conceived approach to astronomy. From this seed point and others, grew my own particular development in teaching, and writing on, astronomy.

Shortly before he died, I had the privilege of meeting Dr. Baravalle in his German nursing home. I also feel it a privilege, with the kind support of Rudolf Steiner College, to be able to edit this little book produced under Dr. Baravalle's authorship, and try to rework it into how I feel he would have wanted to see it.

Norman Davidson
Summer, 1999

Norman Davidson was born in Scotland and was a journalist in the UK for ten years. He became involved with anthroposophy while working as an editor and correspondent in London, and later took the Waldorf Teacher Training course at Emerson College. He was then a Waldorf teacher in England for sixteen years, teaching a variety of subjects in High School and Elementary School, including Geometry, Astronomy and the Legend of Parzival. He emigrated to the USA in 1986 and became Director of Teacher Training at Sunbridge College, New York, until 1998. He still teaches at Sunbridge, and gives courses and lectures elsewhere on a variety of cultural topics. He is the author of *Astronomy and the Imagination* (Arkana/Penguin, UK 1988), and *Sky Phenomena: a Guide to Naked-eye Observation of the Stars* (Lindisfarne Press, Hudson, NY 1993).

Preface

The truly valid introduction to the stars is a walk through open country on a clear night with the gaze turned heavenward. The watcher must be filled with wonder if he or she really looks at what is one of the most awesome spectacles possible in this earthly life. If the contemplative, questioning mood is allowed to prevail, the sky itself answers the questions that arise within the observers as they look.

In words, pictures and charts this book aims to help the answers to come, and the observer to interpret the vast wisdom and mystery which the heavens unfold as they contribute to the human being's enrichment. This book was first written to help teachers present astronomy to sixth-grade children, in keeping with the curriculum of Waldorf schools which were inaugurated by Rudolf Steiner in Stuttgart, Germany, in 1919. This curriculum is now in wide use in Waldorf schools throughout the world. Only later was the material seen to have value for both adults and children seeking to understand the stars, especially those for whom too much technicality was an encumbrance.

In the so-called "space age", in which humans reach out to encounter and even land on what were once termed "heavenly bodies", and cosmic experimentation increases adult interest in "other worlds", it is natural that every schoolchild and many younger ones know of space flights and, for instance, the "weightlessness" of objects being carried in orbit round the earth. "Space ships" and "green men" are part of their armory of toys. Television shows hair-raising, earth-shaking take-offs to the moon; humans moonwalking and floating like feathers in outer space; globe-circling astronauts in fast-spinning orbits controlled from fantastic computer centers—in fact, all the paraphernalia and trappings of today's human-made "miracles" which truly compete with the mysteries of the stars above.

Compete? Yes, but with a difference; perhaps even not with full success! For even these outer-space "miracles" —moon landings, weightlessness, measurements with an accuracy almost beyond human comprehension—are as though dwarfed alongside the still greater miracle, not merely of the stars themselves, but of a child's wonder at them—the astonishment, for example, when an older person pinpoints the "Big Dipper" for the child for the first time.

The young child's first lessons concerning the vast universe are those of night and day. The young child breathes and lives these rhythms. Without any teaching, the child knows day and its sun, night and its moon, and gradually knows those points of light which puncture the night sky's blackness. At first sporadic and imaginative, these youthful interests later become more specific. Only gradually does the time become ready for a systematic study of astronomy. Throughout life, these changes of focus assert themselves according to the character of a person's interests, including an interest in the stars. These interests change like the changes in the sky itself—whimsical like the weather, or orderly like the movements of the stars and planets.

The stars may be not merely studied, but experienced in a way as orderly as their own regularity; and, if so experienced, the stars will in turn transmit this orderliness to the observer who tries to understand them. This book presents the stars as they show themselves directly to experience. Merely cramming the head full of concepts picked up from conversation, articles or popular literature has no place in this work or in any scheme of things based on reality. Such repetitive, mechanical approaches lead to conceit rather than an experience of the stars or of any kind of reverence for the universe. Only a few questions, based on realities of the sky, will then reveal the shallowness of some approaches to astronomy. This book is meant to suggest such realistic questions about the stars.

In this text we show the stars as human-centered and human-experienced. The star charts and diagrams in these pages try to depict phenomena on a hemisphere as seen from within, as people can experience the sky when they look at it. The usual sky representation is just the opposite, showing daily changes in the positions of the stars and constellations in the form of parallel circles, drawn as though seen from without. The gap between these two styles of presentation—the one a picture from without and the other a picture which has meaning only if seen from within, from experience—is not easy to bridge over. And when learning is not experienced from within, it becomes mechanical. People study the "mechanics" of the sky and become lost in it.

The following chapters show the stars as people can really experience them. They are before us, behind us and at the sides. We have but to turn to see them coming in upon us from different directions. These pages attempt to show them as they actually appear—from whatever direction—and bring together the different sky views in a way which activates and sharpens the visualizing power of the observer.

The methods outlined in this book embrace important educational and human values because they stimulate a rich gymnastic of the mind, which systematically strengthens the mental powers.

The student of the stars who utilizes these methods will thus find them an aid to immediate observation of the stars, while at the same time there is built a foundation upon which to trace the findings of astronomy through successive historical epochs. Once the student confronts the actual astronomical phenomena in the heavens, a safe basis is established on which different views and conclusions can come together in the understanding. By developing his or her own powers for observing and thinking about the stars, the student has opened up inwardly and has increased the strength for penetrating the realities of the worlds around.

I Observing the Stars in the Course of a Single Night

People's capacities vary for observing what appears before them. One person may spend a whole night on a fishing boat, and later remember the changing positions of the stars during the night, the rotating movement of the Big Dipper or the rising of a constellation from the horizon. Another person recalls but little.

On top of a mountain at night, perhaps knowing none of the names of the stars or constellations, one may wonder what "fixed stars" are, having somewhere heard the question: Do fixed stars stay in their places, and only planets move? The long-and-short of the matter is that not everyone is an accurate observer. To study the stars, the first requirement is to observe them directly.

Suppose we face the stars to the south of us. For one who does not yet know the stars, a compass may even help to determine which direction is south. A certain bright star shines before us, among many others. It is a certain height above the horizon. Will it stay there at the same spot all night? Or will its position change? The patient observer will see, after not too long a time, that its position is changing. What course does its movement take?

Imagine these observations being reproduced in a classroom. The teacher draws the line of the horizon on the blackboard, with a star above this horizon line, as described above. The teacher lets the students come to the blackboard and draw lines indicating what course they think the star will take when it moves. The resulting lines may sometimes go in almost all directions. These lines on the blackboard alone will make the students realize how much there is for them to learn. Finally, the teacher tells them that after a while the star will be farther to the right. Then, above some point along the horizon line, the teacher locates a star on the blackboard. If this star is to the left in the southern sky, it will rise slightly and proceed to the right. If the star is to the right, it will gradually descend.

Perspective Drawing and Observations of the Stars

In similar manner one might imagine Renaissance artists, like Leonardo da Vinci for example, drawing star paths to investigate perspective. Seated and facing a window, the artist could draw on the window pane with a crayon a picture of the landscape that he saw. By drawing the position of a star on the window pane and doing it repeatedly, for instance half-an-hour later, then one hour later, etc., the artist would obtain the curve of the star's course by thus noting in picture form the star's successive positions and connecting the successive points. One must only take care to keep one's head in the same spot when making the pictures. The curve can also be obtained photographically by exposing film in a camera to the starlight for some hours. Each star will then draw its own course on the film. [Curves thus obtained, which will not be parallel because of their projection onto the plane of the window or film, are shown in Figures 3, 4 and 7. Star paths in Figures 1 and 2 are shown parallel for simplicity, which is also how they can be experienced or conceived in three-dimensional space. Ed.]

Facing the Stars to the South

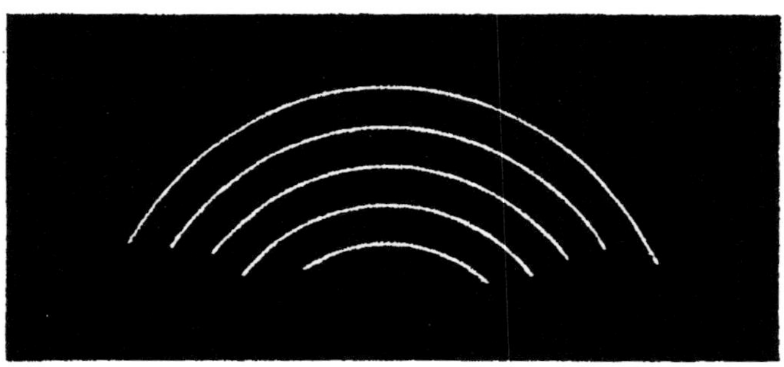

Figure 1. The left-to-right courses of the stars as the observer facing south approximately sees them appear to move above the horizon.

Facing the Stars to the North

Let us now turn the opposite way and face the stars to the north of us. The clear night sky surrounds us, but the picture before us is a wholly different one. The stars above the horizon to the left of due north descend as the night goes on, and those to the right ascend, while those directly above due north on the horizon move toward the right. The further the stars are to the left of due north, the more steeply they descend; and the further they are to the right, the more steeply they ascend.

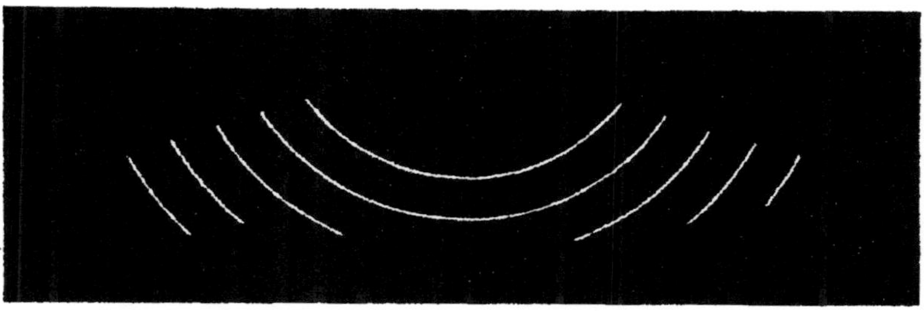

Figure 2. The left-to-right courses of the stars above the horizon as we approximately see them when facing north.

These arcs represent the courses which we see the stars above the northern horizon follow from left to right, with the lower arcs disappearing under the horizon and coming up again— "bathing in the ocean", as the Greeks called this phenomenon, though in our time such manifestations are usually described in concepts rather than pictorially.

Facing the Stars to the East

Now let us face the stars above the horizon to the east of us - that part of the sky in which all stars ascend. From all places in the United States and Europe, we see the stars rise in the eastern sky and move through the night toward the right. We see them ascend more steeply from due east than from the southeast [as when experienced as if on a plane. Ed.]. Figure 3 shows the lines of their daily ascent up from the eastern horizon, when they are projected onto the plane of the page. The line which starts at the due-east horizon point moves straight up into the sky. The lines to the right of that straight, due-east line, form arcs curving away to the right of it; those to the left curve away to the left of it. The straight line is the line of the so-called celestial equator.

Figure 3. The rising courses of the stars from the eastern horizon, projected onto the plane of page.

The straight line of the celestial equator combines the qualities of both a straight line and a circle. It belongs to the geometry of a sphere seen from within. The horizon at sea is a line of this kind. A photograph taken from a ship shows a horizon line as a straight horizontal. Yet we know that this same horizon line runs in front of us, behind us and at both sides of us. We have to turn around to follow it.

Facing the Stars to the West

Let us now look at the western sky. The opposite picture appears before us. In the west, all stars descend. When experienced as if on a plane, those which set exactly at the due west point descend on an inclined straight line. To the right of this line, the courses of the stars are arcs curving in from the right; and to the left of it the stars move in arcs curving in from the left.

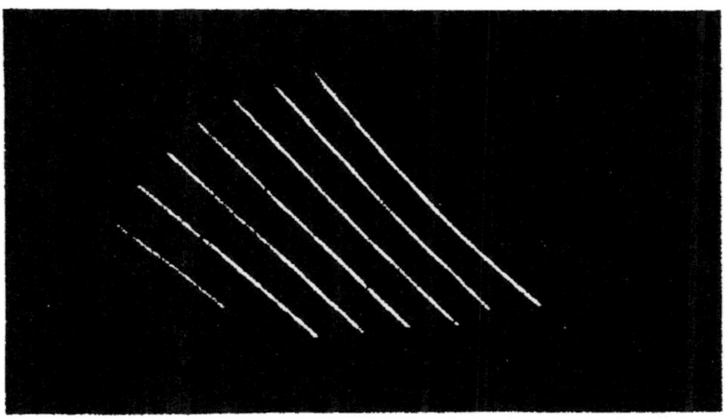

Figure 4. The courses of the stars above the horizon when we face west—projected onto the plane of the page.

The Cupola of the Sky Above Us

With these four major pictures in mind—the celestial scenes which confront us above the horizon as we face south, north, east and west— we may now extend and combine them to form one vast picture filling the entire cupola of the sky above us.

We may first extend the picture of the southern sky, adding to it more and more parallel arcs all the way up to the celestial equator. We now see that the same stars which rise exactly in the east set exactly in the west, their full courses lying along the celestial equator. We may then extend the courses of the stars farther north in the eastern and western sky, lengthening the arcs above the northern horizon far and high above us to the zenith, the point straight over our heads, to form complete circles.

Every single arc—in other words, the course of every single star—can be extended to form a complete circle. The farther north they are, the smaller are these circles. We see them as concentric circles, if seen as if on a flat plane, gradually diminishing in size to their common center (See Figure 5).

This common center is called the celestial pole; the star nearest to it, the Pole Star.

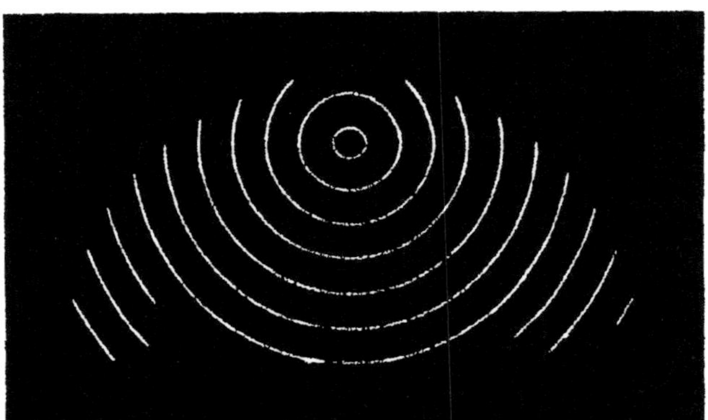

Figure 5. The courses of the stars in the northern sky, seen as if on a flat plane, form concentric circles around the celestial pole.

The Celestial Equator's Center is Within Ourselves

Tracing the circular arcs towards the north, we always find their centers lie on a straight line (axis) passing upwards between us and the north celestial pole. Tracing the arcs above the southern horizon, we find that their centers lie on a line (axis) passing in exactly the opposite direction—downwards toward an opposite pole.

With this picture in mind, we can ask: Where does the celestial equator, which is midway between these two poles, have its center? It does not lie in any direction outside of ourselves. Its center is right within us.

What about the speed of the stars? How fast do they appear to move in their courses? Their relative speed of travel actually varies with position. Stars near the celestial pole move slowly, while those on the celestial equator move the fastest. All the circles—the smallest as well as the largest—are traversed once in the same general time period of a day and a night.

It is possible to measure distances in the sky using handbreadths at arm's length. Measuring vertically upwards from the horizon to the zenith, we come to a distance of about nine handbreadths. Thus one handbreadth represents 90/9, which is 10 degrees. Stars which stand three handbreadths from each other, are about 30 degrees apart.

II Observing the Stars in the Tropical, Arctic and Antarctic Regions

From one part of the earth to another, there appear progressive changes of landscape, climate, plants and animals, and also of the stars in the sky. Even more striking than the beauty and loneliness of the Norwegian fjords are the impressions of the midnight sun, which is above the horizon at midsummer in the far north.

Journeying southward, we see the arcs described by the stars over the southern horizon reach higher and higher. They continue to rise ever more steeply from the eastern horizon, and to descend ever more steeply in the west.

At the equator the arcs rise up vertically from the horizon, and come down vertically to the horizon. Figure 6 shows the curves described by the stars above the southern horizon at this equatorial latitude—all of them semicircles around the due-south horizon point when they are projected onto the plane of the page.

Turning to face north from our standpoint on the equator, we see the same kind of picture of semicircular arcs.

Figure 6. The semicircular courses of the stars as we see them above the southern or northern horizon when we stand at the earth's equator.

Facing east at the equator, the celestial equator (at the center) rises vertically. The arcs to its left and right are circular and rise perpendicularly from the horizon.

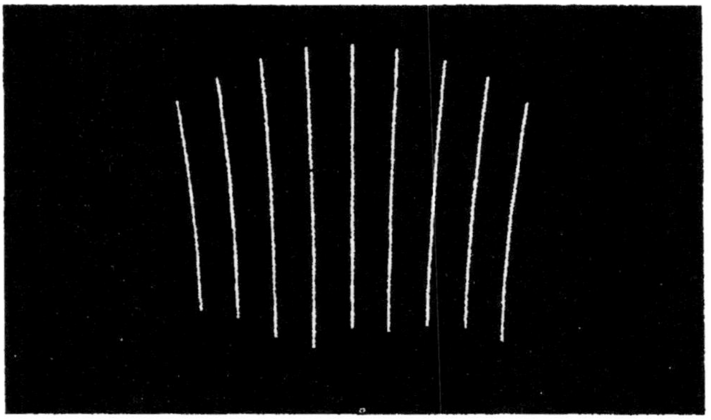

Figure 7. The courses of the stars above the eastern or western horizon when we stand at the earth's equator—as projected onto the plane of the page.

Facing west, we see exactly the same picture, except that the stars no longer rise along these lines, but descend. Because the stars at this equatorial latitude rise and set in a vertical direction, the changes between light and darkness are accordingly more rapid. Because the sun moves more swiftly across the horizon on a path which is at right angles to it and not slanting, morning and evening twilight are shorter and changes of temperature quicker.

The Stars as Seen From Northern and Southern Hemispheres

Conditions generally in the arctic regions are opposite to those at the earth's equator. The stars are no exception. Their courses in the arctic sky show a picture opposite to that seen in tropical skies. Instead of the vertical courses which predominate in the tropics, the horizontal direction prevails in arctic latitudes. At the North Pole all stars proceed above the horizon from left to right without changes in altitude. The celestial equator lies at horizon level, and the Pole Star shines down from near the zenith. Figure 8 pictures the courses of the stars as seen above the horizon at the North Pole. These star courses always take the form of horizontal lines, moving from left to right.

Figure 8. Courses of the stars as we observe them just above the horizon at the North Pole of the earth—all of them being straight horizontals.

At the South Pole the star courses are also all horizontals, except that the stars in the antarctic skies proceed from right to left.

The celestial landscape at the poles harmonizes with the earthly one —wide, snow-covered plains and complete lack of trees or other vertical elements. The gradual transition from the pictures seen in temperate zones to those seen in the tropics and the arctic regions provides challenges for all willing to visualize to themselves this transition as it really occurs. Students can draw pictures of the stars with their respective landscapes. Many drawings made in this way in the

Waldorf school over the years are exercises for the students' imaginations and thinking faculties.

The Southern Hemisphere

In the Southern Hemisphere, the pictures of north and south are just the opposite of the corresponding ones seen in the Northern Hemisphere. A celestial pole can be pictured above the southern horizon with stars circling clockwise round it, while the arc of the sun's path passes over the northern horizon. This reversal is in keeping with the fact that the Frigid Zone is toward the south, the Tropical Zone to the north. The New Zealander goes to the North Island for more sunshine, to the north side of a house for a sunny room.

The stars along the celestial equator appear, of course, to move in exactly the opposite direction to that in which the very same stars appear to move when seen from the Northern Hemisphere. They rise in the east from the right and descend in the west to the left.

III Observing the Night Sky in the Course of a Year

On successive nights over weeks and months, the courses of the stars remain exactly the same, as seen from the same place on earth. Changes occur only concerning the times when, and the places in the sky where, the different star groups are visible. Their appearance and disappearance are observable just before dawn and just after dusk, when the stars are seen rising or setting in relation to the horizon. Before dawn, new star groups after a time are seen rising in the east, as those already risen each morning are to be found increasingly higher in the sky. After dusk, star groups previously seen in the west eventually become no longer visible as they set earlier and earlier on the western horizon.

Corresponding changes are seen to occur at any hour of the night when observations are made over a series of nights. On successive nights, star groups above the eastern horizon are seen to be higher up in the heavens when observed repeatedly at the same hour. In the west, star groups are found nearer to the horizon as the nights go on. Facing the south, one observes the star groups progressing always toward the west as time passes.

Methods used for studying the stars' nightly courses can be used to assess their movements over a longer period. Photographs of the night sky may be taken at the same hour and in the same direction on successive nights. This would show the nightly movement of the stars during a year. But to take such photographs every two hours on the same night would be roughly equivalent to photographing the sky every month at the same time of night. The successive positions of the stars from hour to hour on the same night, joined together, will picture the curves of their motion during the year. For the southern or the northern, the eastern or the western sky, the curves pictured for the advancing year repeat those for the advancing night. In the course of a year a star observed at the same time of night disappears to the west and reappears in the east to return approximately to the position it started from. In the course of a single day and night, the same star moves round this same circle. The following approximate correspondences are thus seen to exist in the changes of the positions of the stars over the twelve months of the year and over the twenty-four hours of the day:

Daily changes	**Yearly changes**
24 hours	12 months
2 hours	1 month
1 hour	2 weeks
½ hour	1 week
4 minutes	1 day

How Clocks Tell Star Time in Astronomical Observatories

A star, observed at the same moment on two successive nights, is seen to have shifted its position toward the west by just under 4 minutes when the movement is measured in terms of ordinary clock time which is based on the mean movement of the sun. Small as the nightly change may seem, its cumulative increase over longer periods becomes significantly large. After only a month, the change in star positions for, say, 10 o'clock is seen to be about as much as during two hours on a single night. A star on the celestial equator changes its position about 15 degrees (1 ½ handbreadths) in one hour; in two hours, about 30 degrees (three handbreadths). Corresponding changes take place in the yearly cycle every two weeks and every month respectively. The change in the night sky from Christmas midnight to Christmas at 2 a.m. will be roughly the same as from midnight of December 24 to midnight of January 24. The view of the stars at midnight on December 24 will be seen at 8 p.m. two months later.

The whole Christmas midnight sky reappears earlier and earlier in the evenings in spring until its last appearance after sunset in March. Then, as a whole, it can be seen before sunrise again in the early morning sky in the fall. Any aspect of the starry sky, any constellation of the zodiac, first becomes visible before sunrise, and is last seen after sunset.

Astronomical observatories use sidereal clocks which run differently from ordinary clocks. Sidereal clocks tell "star time". They follow the circling of the stars and move faster westwards than the (mean) sun by just under 4 minutes each day (more precisely, 3.94 minutes), or by about 24 hours in a year. Zero hours by sidereal time is when the spring equinox point is due south. Zero hours by ordinary clock time (mean solar time) is when the sun is in the north (midnight). So sidereal time and ordinary clock time coincide only once a year around the AUTUMNAL equinox in September. Using star time, it is possible to set up convenient tables for locating the stars and for listing the times of their risings and settings.

IV Observing the Sun in the Course of the Day and in the Course of the Year

Ask anyone how much time it takes for the sun to set—in other words, from the time when its disc first touches the horizon until it completely disappears—and the answer may be "one minute" or "a half-hour" or any time span between these two. If the questioner is a teacher dealing with students, he or she may note down the answers, then ask the students to check their answers by actually observing a sunset and report their findings the following day.

For places in the United States and in most of Europe, it takes the sun around three minutes to set, depending upon geographical latitude—longer the farther north the observer goes, shorter in the south. At the equator, the setting time is about two minutes.

At what locations on the horizon line does the sun rise and set? Does the whole course of the sun from rising to setting correspond with the curves of the courses of the stars as described above? Yes, it does.

After the sun has set and darkness has come, an afterglow of daylight is still visible on the western horizon—first lighter, gradually more faded, but still perceptible for a long time after sunset. This afterglow appears in a limited area within an arc above the horizon. Continuing this arc to round out an imagined circle of which it is a part, then locating the circle's center, one discovers this center to be a point under the horizon; also that this center point does not remain fixed as the hours go by, but gradually moves from the west toward the north. The light shines from the sun, which is continuing its course under the horizon.

The moving center point thus established marks the changing position of the sun after setting. In northern countries, a shining of this kind is visible all night in summer. From the sunset point on the horizon, this afterglow gradually moves northward, and at midnight stands in the north itself. After midnight it moves northeastward, then to the east, until its center is finally at the point on the eastern horizon where the sun rises.

The Sun's Course

It is also possible to observe not only the sun's daily, but its yearly course. In summer the sun rises in the northeast, sets in the northwest, and at noon is high in the southern sky. The observer can see its course changing as summer progresses, and see the changed position within the range of the arcs shown in the picture of the eastern heavens (Figure 3, left side).

In winter we observe the sun's course again changing within the range of the arcs shown in the east to the right of the celestial equator (Figure 3, right side), and stretching lower in the southern sky. In March (around the 21st) and in September (around the 23rd) the sun's course through the sky follows the celestial equator.

As summer approaches, it is seen to move upward day by day from the celestial equator to ever higher arcs, reaching its highest position on about June 22. After that date the sun's course moves downward again, reaching the celestial equator in September and its lowest position of the year on about December 21, the time of the shortest days and the longest nights.

In the temperate zone in winter, when day can break at 8 a.m. and darkness come again at 4 p.m., the day consists of only eight daylight hours and sixteen dark hours. One-third of the twenty-four-hour day is light, and two-thirds dark. Also, at this time of winter, only one-third of the sun's daily path is above the horizon; two-thirds are below the horizon.

At the geographic latitude of 45 degrees north, half-way between the North Pole and the earth's equator (this latitude passes through the state of Maine in the eastern United States; Oregon in the west; and northern Italy in Europe), it is possible to picture very specifically the sun's arc of travel through the sky. The celestial equator passes from the due-east horizon point to the due-west horizon point, passing along a path 45 degrees above the due-south horizon point - that is, a path passing half-way between this horizon point and the zenith. And close to half the distance between the celestial equator's due south position and the horizon lies the position of the sun at the depth of winter (23.4 degrees below the celestial equator). At the height of summer, the sun's path is exactly the same distance above the celestial equator. Through the spring months the sun mounts higher and higher above the southern horizon until it reaches this peak height close to half-way between the celestial equator and the zenith (23.4 degrees above the celestial equator).

The lengthening of the days from December to June does not proceed in equal steps. It begins very slowly around Christmas, then gradually speeds up, continuing until March, when it is quickest. Thereafter the days lengthen more slowly. In later summer they shorten again, becoming shorter fastest in September and shortening continuously thereafter through the first half of December - the speed of change going from slow in the summer to quick and finally to slow again in the winter.

Lengthening and Shortening of Days

To follow most clearly the changes in the sun's daily path through the sky with the lengthening and shortening of the days, it is best to observe repeatedly, day after day, the sun's midday position. At a geographical latitude of 45 degrees, its path changes within the range of about one-quarter to three-quarters of the distance between the due-south horizon point and the zenith. The sun's path is seen to be mounting, first slowly, then more quickly, then slowly again, from its low winter position to its high summer position. And the return of the sun from its high summer position to its low winter position follows the same pattern of change in pace from slow to faster and again to slower. A musical chord vibrates according to the same mathematical law of changing pace. It is called harmonic motion, and also applies to the speed of movement of a pendulum or a swing.

Every shadow made by the sun follows a course of movements which repeat in their own way the daily path of the sun itself. One has but to put up a rod two or three feet high to observe that even in a few minutes' time a mark indicating the tip of the shadow of the rod upon the ground will have to be changed to keep up with the moving shadow. Similarly, a pencil erected vertically on a horizontal drawing board will throw a shadow whose end point gradually traces a curve on the board (Figure 9). This curve reflects two kinds of motion. One is the rotation of the shadow around the rod; the other is the change between longer and shorter shadows.

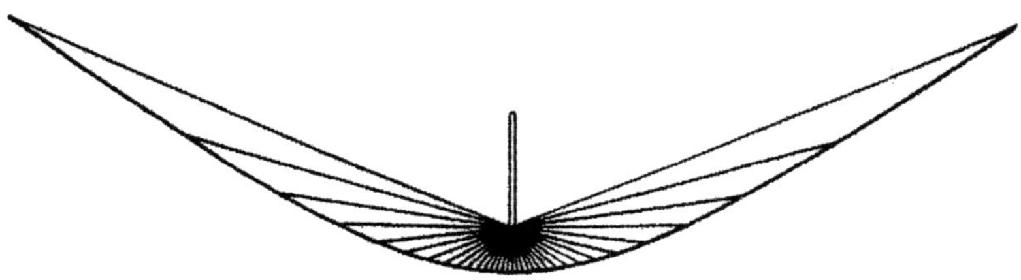

Figure 9. The movement and changing length of the shadow of a vertical rod on a sunlit horizontal surface, repeats in its own way the daily path of the sun.

Before sunset and immediately after sunrise, all shadows are long. While the sun is in the east, all shadows point to the west. When the sun arrives over the southern horizon, all shadows point to the north. When the sun is in the west, all shadows turn from the north to the east. The curve described by a shadow's end point (particularly at latitudes between the arctic and antarctic circles) is a hyperbola. These hyperbolae change through the course of the year. Figure 10 shows the month-to-month changes in the curves traced by the end point of the shadow of a rod. ("A" in Figure 10 marks the rod seen from above).

Among these hyperbolae forms is a straight line, described by the shadow's end point in March and September, when the sun's course lies along the celestial equator. The great circle, with us as center which the sun itself now draws in the heavens, is seen as a straight line in the shadow on the ground. In Figure 10, three curves are drawn above the straight-line stage and three below. The curves above the straight line lie closer to the rod.

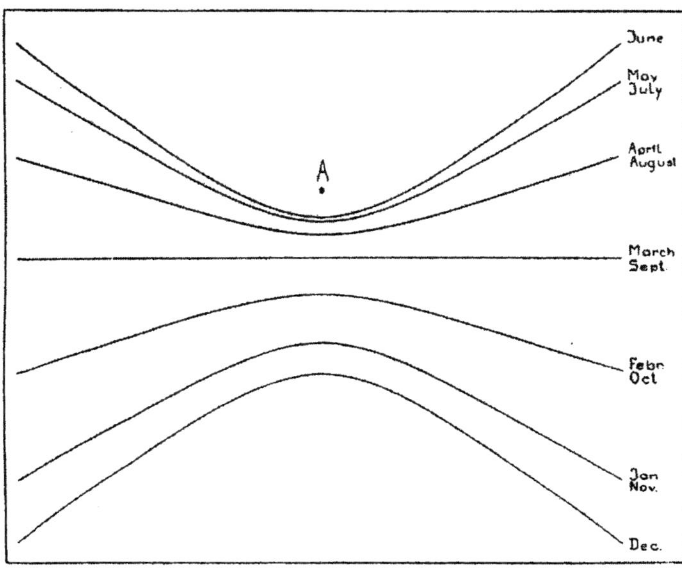

Figure 10. Shadow hyperbolae drawn from month to month by the end point of the shadow of a rod (Point A) erected vertically upon a horizontal surface.

The lines closer to the rod are drawn during the time of shorter shadows, during the half year of the summer. The one immediately above the straight line is the curve for April; the next, for May; the third, for June. There are also three curves below the straight line. They lie farther away from the rod, and represent the months of longer shadows, the half year of the winter. The hyperbolae of the half year of the summer close in around the rod; those of the half year of the winter turn away from it. These contrasting curves are projections of the contrast between the different seasonal arcs of the sun's movement through the sky.

V Observing the Sun in the Tropical, Arctic and Antarctic Regions

The observer who follows the courses of the different stars in the sky can see that the courses of those near the celestial equator can be traced also by the sun at different times of the year—a fact that is true at any geographical latitude or in any country on earth.

At the earth's equator, the celestial equator can be imagined rising up perpendicularly from the eastern horizon, proceeding directly overhead, then descending perpendicularly to the western horizon. The sun follows this same course around March 21 and around September 23. At those times the sun stands at midday in the zenith, and can be seen to shine straight down into, say, a well. When the sun is directly overhead, a vertical rod casts no shadow.

From the earth's equator, the celestial equator is experienced as being the mid-position which the sun's path reaches in the course of the year. If one stands facing east at the equator on earth, the sun's daily course is seen to lie to the left of the celestial equator during the half year containing June, to the extent of 23.4 degrees at its fullest swing in that direction, and to lie correspondingly far to the right of the celestial equator during the half year containing December. This 23.4-degree arc can be measured along the eastern horizon from the due-east point to the points where the sun comes up at sunrise in December or June, or again along the western horizon from the due-west point to the points where the sun goes down at sunset at the solstices.

The sun's yearly movement, as seen from the earth's equator, can also be measured at noon by its distance from the zenith. In June and

December alike it does not reach the zenith, and its course lies 23.4 degrees below the zenith at its low points in these months. At both these times, from the earth's equator, the sun is seen to stand at noon equally high above the horizon. In these months, the height of the sun above the horizon at noon is the same. Consequently, at these two opposite periods of the year, at the earth's equator, it is equally warm and equally light. In fact, there is at the equator no difference between December and June.

Perpendicular Rising and Setting—The Semicircular Course

At the earth's equator, when the daily ascent of the sun is perpendicular in the east and its descent perpendicular in the west, its path is seen to be a semicircle reaching over the sky from east to west. Day and night are close to equal in length. Sunrise is around 6 a.m., sunset around 6 p.m. There are twelve hours in a day and twelve hours in a night. The rhythm of the day has achieved the maximum regularity, but the rhythm of the year has lost its significance. Of the two main rhythms of our lives (those of day and year), the rhythm of the day here takes over.

At or near the equator, the change of temperature between day and night can be greater than between the yearly extremes. It is very different in the north Temperate Zone, where the weather may be expected to change more drastically with the course of the year, bringing beautiful autumns and clear October days, say, in New York, and snow in the first months of the year.

In tropical countries, even the weather can change with the day's rhythm, with perhaps sunshine in the mornings, clouds between 1 and 2 p.m., pouring rain between 2 and 3 p.m., and clear sky and sunshine at 4:30 p.m.

At the Earth's Poles

What is true of the sky in the arctic regions is clearly expressed at the North Pole. In fact, conditions at both of the earth's poles represent to a larger or smaller degree those prevailing throughout the whole of the arctic or antarctic region, whichever it may be.

The movement of the stars at the poles is horizontal (see Figure 8). So is the daily movement of the sun. The celestial equator at the poles is at horizon level; so is the path of the sun in March and September. Half of the sun's daily trips through the sky take place below the horizon. The sun actually remains below the horizon for half a year; that is the time of the polar night. For some days it is at sunrise level. Then, because its ascending daily motion is in an apparent spiral, its path appears again above the horizon. The sun rises to about 23.4 degrees above the horizon in June at the North Pole, and to the same height above the horizon in December at the South Pole. The highest summer positions of the sun in both polar regions are approximately the same distance above the horizon as the lowest winter positions are below the horizon.

The Rhythm of the Day and the Rhythm of the Year

In the polar regions, sunrise does not occur within the day's rhythm as it is known in the temperate zones. At the poles, the day's rhythm has been taken over by the rhythm of the year.

Only one sunrise per year takes place at the poles, and that is in the spring. And the only sunset is in the fall. Light and darkness, too, no longer change with the day in the frozen north, but with the year. There is no obvious maximum midday height of the sun. The sun is close to being equally high at morning, at evening and even at midnight.

In northern Norway I was surprised to hear that the predominance of the year over the day extends deeply even into human life. Fishermen in these regions remain awake for twenty-four hours in summer, with no more than a kind of afternoon rest. Throughout the whole summer, the Eskimos gather in provisions for winter, whereas in the tropics life proceeds from day to day. In the winter the opposite condition prevails in the arctic regions, with the rhythm of the year predominating and its distinctive characteristics supplanting those of the rhythm of the day.

What do we learn from these rhythms?

In the tropics, day takes over. The year is less significant.

In the arctic regions, the year takes over. The day is less significant.

Such observations induce observers to reflect upon their own lives, upon the rhythms of humanity, and to realize that if they live in the temperate zones they have most likely accepted the days and the years as a matter of course without reflecting upon what conditions there are in another region of the world, where either the rhythm of the year or the rhythm of the day almost exclusively prevails.

VI Observing the Moon as a Pointer to the Sun

The moon's aspects for the observer are most varied. At full moon one sees the complete disk; at other times, half disks or various crescent forms. Normally the sun is seen as a full disk, the stars as points of light. Only the moon appears in these varying shapes.

Whether at full moon, or at half-disk moons, or at crescent moons, one-half of the total surface of the moon is always lighted by the sun, while one-half is in darkness. Sometimes we are facing the lighted side; at other times, more or less of the dark side. When the moon appears as a half disk, we are facing half of its light side and half of its dark side. At the time of the slender crescents, only a little of the light side and much of the dark side are toward us.

A crescent moon shows two borderlines. One is the edge of the moon's disk; the other, the line separating the lighted side from the dark side. If one imagines the border between the lighted side and the dark side continuing all the way around the moon, half of it visible and half invisible, one pictures the two halves together projecting into an elliptical form.

Figure 11. When imagining the borderline between lighted and dark portions of the moon's disk to be continued all the way around the moon, one pictures an elliptical form.

When we see the moon as a half disk, the ellipse flattens to a straight line. When the moon is full, the ellipse widens to the full circle of the moon, coinciding with its outer edge. In Figure 11, an arrow is drawn from the center of the moon through the middle of its lighted side. This arrow points in the direction from which the sun's light comes to it and illuminates it.

Figure 12 shows a half-disk moon aspect. The border separating the lighted portion from the dark is seen as a straight line. Perpendicular to this line is the arrow pointing to the sun. At full moon, such an arrow has to be drawn from its center and in our direction. This arrow, prolonged, would extend to behind us where the sun stands. For there beyond us, on the opposite side of the earth, is the sun when the moon is full. We, as observers on the earth, are then somewhere between the moon and the sun.

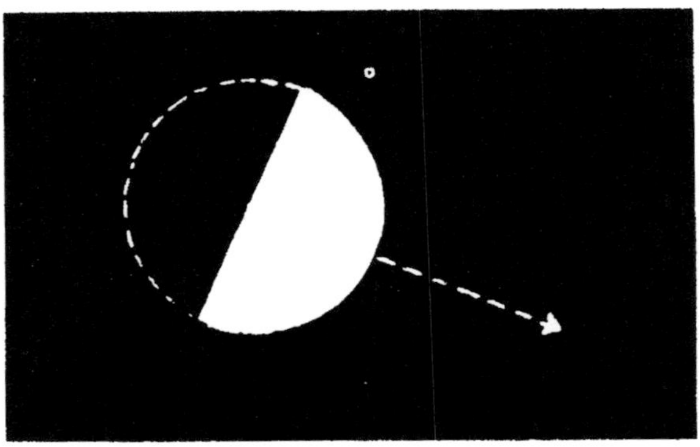

Figure 12. The line separating the lighted and dark portions of the disk of a half moon is seen as a straight line.

The Moon Shows the Position of the Sun

Whenever the moon is visible in the sky, it tells us the position of the sun. With the moon as guide, the observer can follow the course of the sun under the horizon.
When the full moon is rising in the east, the sun is setting in the west, on the other side of the horizon from the moon. During the first evening hours, when the full moon is rising above the eastern horizon, the sun is descending correspondingly low under the western horizon. At midnight, when the full moon stands above the southern horizon, the sun is under the northern horizon.

In winter, when the sun follows a lower daily course, which brings it at night far below the horizon, the full moon rides high in the sky. In summer, when the sun takes a higher daily course, which brings it less far below the horizon at night, the full moon rises about as high in the south as the winter sun.

The observer may read from the moon the direction of the sun's position. Simply by stretching out an arm to mark a line from the center of the moon through the middle of its lighted side (see arrow, Figure 11), the observer will be pointing in the direction of a spot below which the sun then stands. Broadly speaking, when the dividing line separating the moon's lighted portion from its dark portion is in a vertical position, and the lighted outer arc of the moon curves to the right, the sun at that time is setting on the western horizon, while the moon itself is around its highest position in the southern sky. During the first half of the night, the moon so aspected is descending to the west (Figure 12) and it sets around midnight. As it descends, the dividing line between its visible lighted portion and its dark portion gradually changes from a vertical to a horizontal position, and the half disk of the moon gradually becomes like a cup opening upward.

At other times, when the dividing line between the moon's lighted and its dark portions is again vertical, but with its lighted half disk to the left, an arm outstretched in the direction of the sun points horizontally to the left. In general, the sun at such a time is rising on the eastern horizon, while the moon is around its highest position in the southern sky. At such a time, during the first half of the day, the moon is descending toward the west and is seen in daylight until it sets around noon. During that same half day, an arrow drawn perpendicular to the line dividing its lighted from its shadowed portions points increasingly upwards. This change occurs during daytime hours as the sun moves higher in the sky, but is clearly observable. For some days every month the moon is visible for such daytime observation.

The Crescent Moon

The moon's "sickle" or crescent shapes can also tell the sun's position. What is wrong, for instance, in Figure 13?

Figure 13. What is wrong with this picture?

When the moon's crescent is tilted as in this picture, the arrow drawn to point in the direction of the sun would have to point upward. The sun would be high above the horizon; it would then be day, and the stars could not be seen.

The moon's crescents stand above the horizon shortly before sunrise and shortly after sunset. When a crescent moon appears before sunrise, it is always on the eastern horizon. The arrow (as shown in Figure 11) points to the left and downward, indicating the general position of the sun which is still below the horizon. When later the sun rises, the crescent is curved more upward toward the left and the arrow indicates the direction beneath which the sun appears on the eastern horizon. As the sun mounts higher and higher above the horizon, the crescent takes on the aspect of a cup overturned with the arrow pointing upward in the direction of the sun.

In the evening sky, the crescent moon appears only in the west, curved to the right (in the Northern Hemisphere) or downward. It remains visible for only a short time after sundown and the thinner the crescent the briefer the period of its visibility.

The full moon is visible all night long; the half moon about half the night; the crescents for only small portions of the night. When the full-moon stage has passed, the moon gradually disappears from the evening sky. It disappears in two ways: Its lighted portion slowly becomes smaller and smaller; and it illuminates the night sky for ever briefer and briefer lengths of time.

The stars, the sun and the moon all follow the daily paths indicated in Figures 1,3 and 4. But only the sun's path is in step with the rhythm of the day. From day to day, for example (in terms of movement from east to west), the stars rise progressively ahead of the sun, while the moon lags behind the sun.

In the evening, a crescent moon is only seen in the western sky. It sets around 50 minutes later on each successive evening, thus remaining visible for a longer time, while simultaneously its lighted portion grows larger each night until it reaches the half-disk and later the full-moon stages.
In the morning, the crescent moon is only seen in the eastern sky, where it rises before the sun. It rises later every morning, the time of its visibility shortening until it disappears in the light of the rising sun.

The time after the crescent moon's disappearance from the morning sky is the time of the "dark of the moon," and its reappearance in the evening sky marks the time of the waxing crescent moon, the start of a new moon cycle, during which the thin crescent grows larger and larger as the moon lingers longer behind the setting sun.

Because the stars, on the contrary, move daily progressively ahead of the sun from east to west, a star first appears briefly in the morning, rising more and more ahead of the sun and thus remaining visible for more and more of the night before the sun rises. At length the star is rising in the east as the sun is setting from the previous day, and is shining all night before finally disappearing westwards from the evening sky into the sunset. The return to its first appearance in the morning takes one year to complete.

The moon does exactly the reverse. Because the moon lingers increasingly behind the sun's daily movement, each crescent moon appears in the evening after sunset, growing in light and duration from night to night until it becomes a full moon. Afterwards it is visible over shorter periods, and eventually only for the second half of the night; then finally only very briefly before it vanishes entirely in the light of the rising sun. Its return to its first appearance in the evening takes one lunar month to complete.

Summary

1. The crescent moon, curved to the right, is visible in the evening, setting in the first hours of the night.

2. The moon's half disk, curved to the right, is visible in the evening and through the first half of the night, setting around midnight.

3. The full moon, rising in the evening, setting at sunrise, is visible the whole night long.

4. The moon's half disk, curved to the left, rising around midnight, is visible through the second half of the night, setting around midday.

5. The crescent moon, curved now to the left, rising in the last hours of the night, can remain visible in the sky during the day.

VII Observing the Planets—Flexibility in the Cosmos

Five "stars", different from all the others, appear at times in the night sky. All five shine brightly at night in some months, but during others can hardly be seen, or cannot be seen at all. These five special stars include the brightest of all stars, the morning star and the evening star—which are actually one and the same star, appearing sometimes before sunrise and at other times after sunset.

This brightest of stars is Venus.

Not only does the light of these five special stars vary, but their positions among the other stars vary, too.

Of all the stars in the sky, other than these five special ones, we may imagine a triangle made up of any three of them, and observe this triangle night after night without discovering any change in its form. The triangle is sometimes higher in the night sky, sometimes lower; the triangle turns; but it always retains the same form. Yet if one of the other five special stars becomes one of the three points of the triangle, then the triangle is seen to move into many forms, because this "special" star, this one of "the five", does not follow the pattern of movement common to all the other stars in the sky.

These five special stars are therefore what can be called "wandering stars" or planets. In contrast to them, all the other stars are called "fixed stars". The word "fixed" refers to their positions with respect to each other, not to any fixed altitude nor permanent, immovable position.

Three of these planets may appear at any hour of the night. The other two are never seen at midnight in mid-northern latitudes; they appear at these latitudes only in the morning and evening sky. The three planets which may appear all night long are Mars, Jupiter and Saturn. Those two which are seen mostly in the morning and evening skies are Venus and Mercury. [From far northern and southern latitudes it is possible to see Venus or Mercury at midnight too, at times when the sun does not descend very far beneath the horizon in the middle of the night. Ed.]

Jupiter

The brightest of those first three planets which may appear all night long is Jupiter. When Jupiter shines all night, it rises evening after evening among the same group of fixed stars. Repeated observation, night after night, will show its position among them, however, to be shifting even after a week; more obviously after a month.

Jupiter may, for instance, have progressed, in relation to the fixed stars, a short distance to the right. Then continuing observations over several months may reveal this progression to the right to reverse itself, so that Jupiter is seen to be moving in the very opposite direction to the left.

Figure 14 shows Jupiter's movement in 1977. From January until the summer of that year Jupiter was in the star group of Taurus. It moved to the right until the middle of January, when it turned to the left. In early June it was together with the sun in the sky, and therefore invisible for a time. In August it moved into Gemini. Toward the end of the year, in late October, it started again to reverse its direction of movement, proceeding once more to the right and so continuing even further to the right than it had at the beginning of the year. Still later its course moved again to the left.

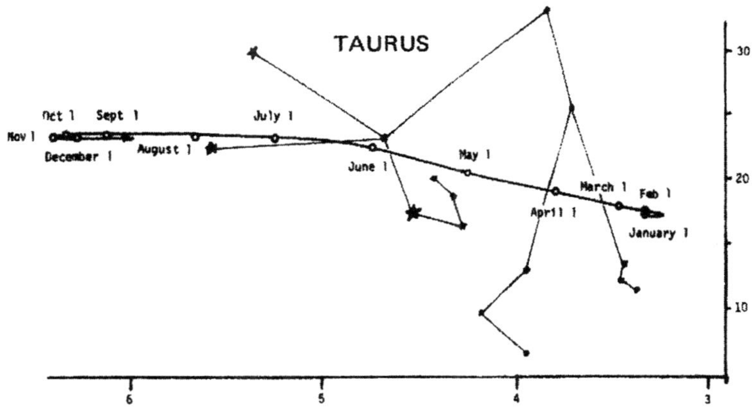

Figure 14. Movement of Jupiter in 1977.

The numerals on the vertical line at the right in Figure 14 show numbers of degrees above the celestial equator, and those along the horizontal celestial equator at the bottom of the diagram indicate 15-degree steps eastwards from the spring equinox point. If at a given moment the point marked "4" is above "due south", the point marked "5" will be at that position an hour later.

Mars

Mars, too, is seen from time to time for extended nocturnal periods, shining brightly and slightly reddish in the night sky. Its position among the surrounding stars is also seen to shift if repeatedly observed night after night. Its changes are even greater than those of Jupiter.

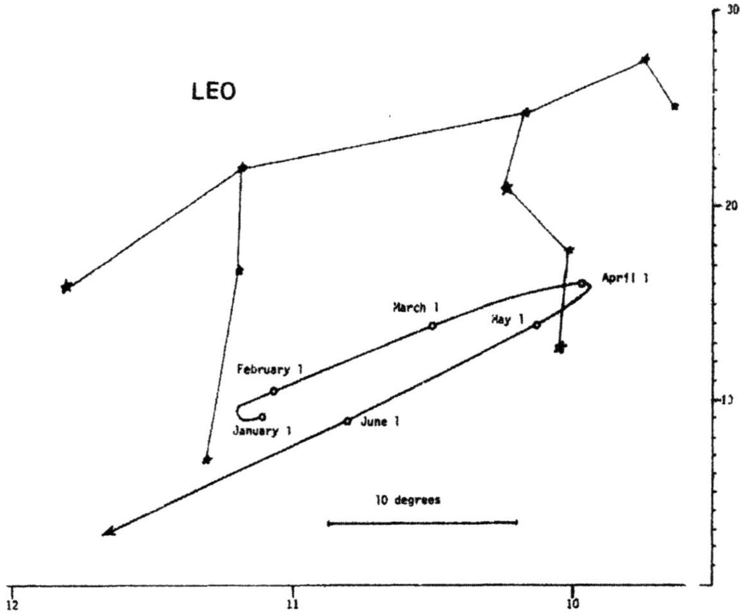

Figure 15. Positions of Mars in the first half of 1980.

Figure 15 shows the positions of Mars in the first half of 1980, when the planet cuts a picturesque curve in the constellation of Leo. At the beginning of that year the path of Mars moves to the left; in the middle of January it turns to the right, until in April it curves again to the left. In May and June it moves farther and farther to the left.

To the left of Leo is the constellation of Virgo. Both these star groups belong to the twelve constellations comprising what is called the zodiac. When Mars continues on its course to the left, it passes through all twelve zodiacal groups which extend in a vast ring around the full circle of the sky. Then Mars will pass again through Leo.

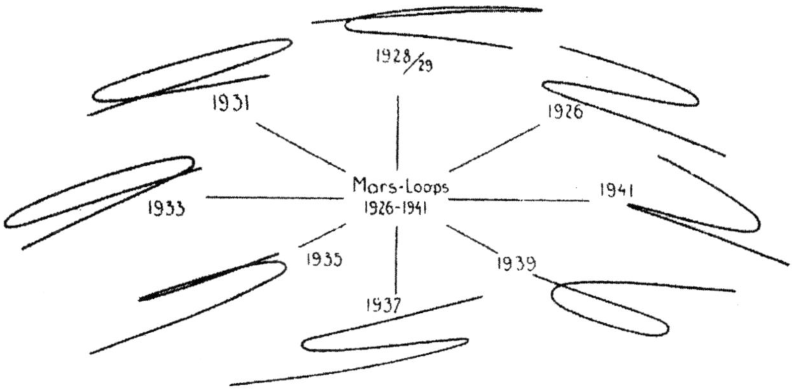

Figure 16. The curves of Mars from 1926 to 1941, showing the orderly development of their metamorphosis.

The curve of the path of Mars is different every year. Figure 16 shows the Mars curves from 1926 to 1941. The sequence started with an open "Z" form in 1926. In 1928/29 the form shifted to a narrow loop. The loop widened in 1931 and 1933, then narrowed again in 1935. Then in 1937 the path of Mars again became an open form, this time in the shape of an "S." The loop turned downward in 1939, and for 1941 was a transition from that downward loop to an open "Z" type of form.

This sequence is characteristic not only of the path of Mars, but also of that of Jupiter. Jupiter, however, performs loops which are just over a year apart, and they are smaller and closer together.

The loops of Saturn are still smaller, narrower, and more frequent.

Venus and Mercury

The other two planets, Venus and Mercury, which appear mostly in the morning and evening, are always seen in the vicinity of the sun; either a little closer or a little farther away from it. They either precede the sunrise in the morning, appearing to the right of the sun, or else they follow the sunset, when they appear to the sun's left. Whether Venus is to the west (right) or to the east (left) of the sun, determines whether it is the morning or evening star.

Figure 17 shows the positions of Venus in relation to the sun (the horizontal line representing the sun's daily path) in 1977. At the beginning of that year Venus stood far to the left of the sun. Because its position was at the same time higher than the sun (further north towards the pole on the celestial sphere), Venus was at that time in good visibility as the evening star. At the beginning of April, Venus was close to the sun and invisible in its light, and it was close to the sun and invisible again at the end of the year.

Figure 17. Positions of Venus in relation to the sun in 1977.

Most of the year, Venus was seen as a morning star. It was not, however, in very good visibility in May and June, being further south than the sun (below its daily path) on the celestial sphere. Figure 17 shows the length of 10 degrees, to which the diagram is scaled (equivalent of a handbreadth as seen in the sky), and makes it possible to judge the planet's distance from the sun at different times. Throughout the year, Venus is never farther than five handbreadths from the sun.

The curve of Venus is different from appearance to appearance, showing even greater variety than the curves of Mars, Jupiter and Saturn. Depending upon its curve, Venus's visibility varies. In some years it is to be seen a great deal, both as the morning and as the evening star; in other years its visibility is less favorable. When its visibility in the United States and in Europe is poor, it is much more to be seen in the Southern Hemisphere, where its prominence is the reverse of what it is at latitudes north of the equator.

Mercury, being still closer to the sun, is therefore visible only at dawn and dusk. If it is to the right of the sun, it is a morning star; if to the left, it is an evening star. Its visibility changes much more frequently than that of Venus. Venus passed the sun (either from left to right or from right to left) once in 1977; Mercury passed it six times in 1979.

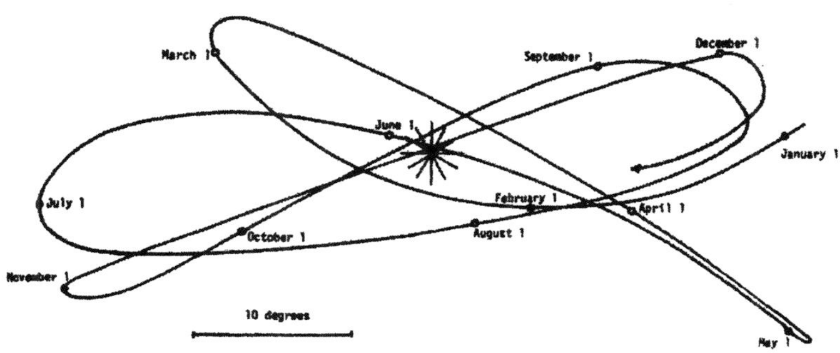

Figure 18. Positions of Mercury in relation to the sun in 1979.

Figure 18 shows, in a similar way to Figure 17 for Venus, the positions of Mercury in relation to the sun in 1979. The distance of 10 degrees on this scale (a handbreadth as seen in the sky) is indicated below the diagram. From this unit of measure as a guide, it is seen that Mercury remained always within 30 degrees of the sun in that year.
Its curves form three loops to the left and three loops to the right in the course of a year. Some loops are more rounded, as the middle loop to the left; some are narrower, like the loop to the right downward. Some loops are longer, others shorter.

Figure 19 shows Mercury's loops for the following year.

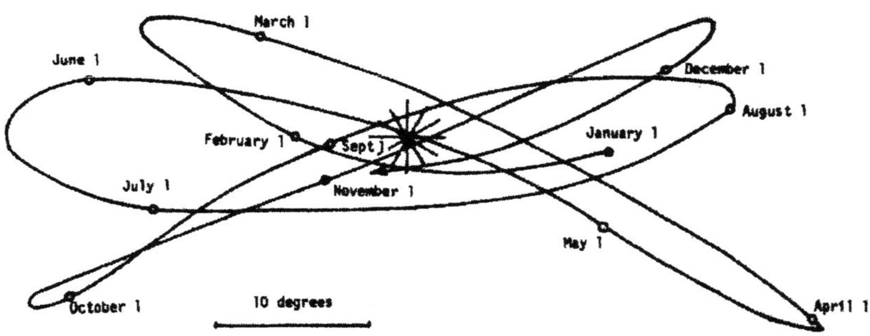

Figure 19. Positions of Mercury in relation to the sun in 1980.

Comparing Figures 18 and 19 shows numerous changes from one year to the next. The loop in Figure 18 to the right downward becomes more round in Figure 19. The two upper left loops of Figure 18 come closer together in Figure 19, etc.

The times of Mercury's best visibility can be derived from such a diagram, taking the celestial sphere's relationship to the horizon of one's geographical latitude into account. At mid-northern latitudes in 1980, for instance, it is best seen as a morning star in the second half of November, and as an evening star in mid-February. At these times, Mercury is higher than the sun, as well as relatively separate from it to west or east and therefore least likely to be obscured by the sun's brightness.

Mercury's best visibility of all in 1980 is in the Southern Hemisphere, where visibility is the reverse of what it is in the Northern Hemisphere. Its best morning visibility for the Southern Hemisphere is in the first half of April; its best evening visibility, the first half of October.

To the observer marking the sun's positions above the southern horizon at noon by the clock (i.e., using "mean" solar time) day after day throughout the year, not only its rising and falling are evident, but also another kind of movement is seen. At some times of the year the actual sun (marking the observed, "apparent" solar time) has already passed due south at mean noon by the clock and stands slightly to the right of that point. At other times of the year the actual sun has not yet reached due south at mean noon, and stands to its left.

The sun's observed position at mean noon, day after day, progressively follows the form of a "figure 8," or lemniscate (see Figure 20). The horizontal straight line shows the celestial equator, and the mark at its center indicates the direction of due south. Half of the "8"-shaped curve is above, and half below, the celestial equator. Photographs of the sun at noon by the clock, taken each day on the same film, would show the "figure 8" form being completed after one full year.

If it were possible to include Mercury in these "mean-noon" photographs of the sun, they would show this planet not only going high with the sun in summer and low with the sun in winter, but also following a looping curve from left to right of the sun. Figure 20 shows this curve for 1979. Following the direction of the arrow, this Mercury curve starts in low winter positions, then rises by mid-March to a level of about 6 ½ degrees above the celestial equator, afterward drops again until April, then performs its major rise from April until June. In this major rise, Mercury advances with the sun in April and May as the sun lifts in the sky to its summer height.

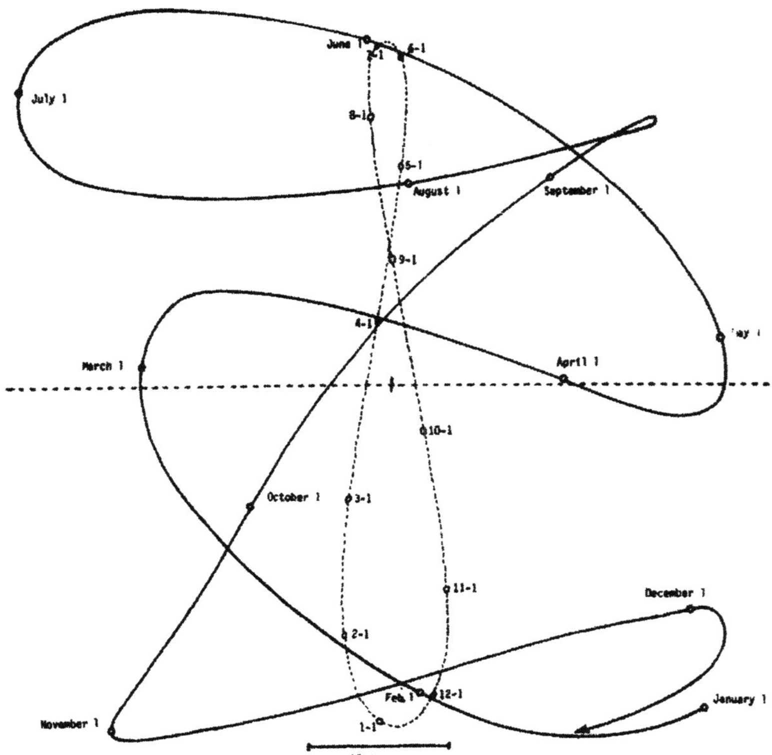

Figure 20. Mercury's path follows a close relationship to that of the sun, above and below the celestial equator (horizontal line), in summer and winter respectively, throughout the year. Its 1979 curve is shown here, along with the lemniscate of the sun's mean noon position.

Mercury reaches a second maximum altitude in the middle of August, then rapidly descends until November 1. After another rise throughout November to the beginning of December, Mercury drops to its winter low later in December. This type of curve, showing Mercury's successive positions at a given time each day, most effectively suggests its quick mobility through the course of a single year.

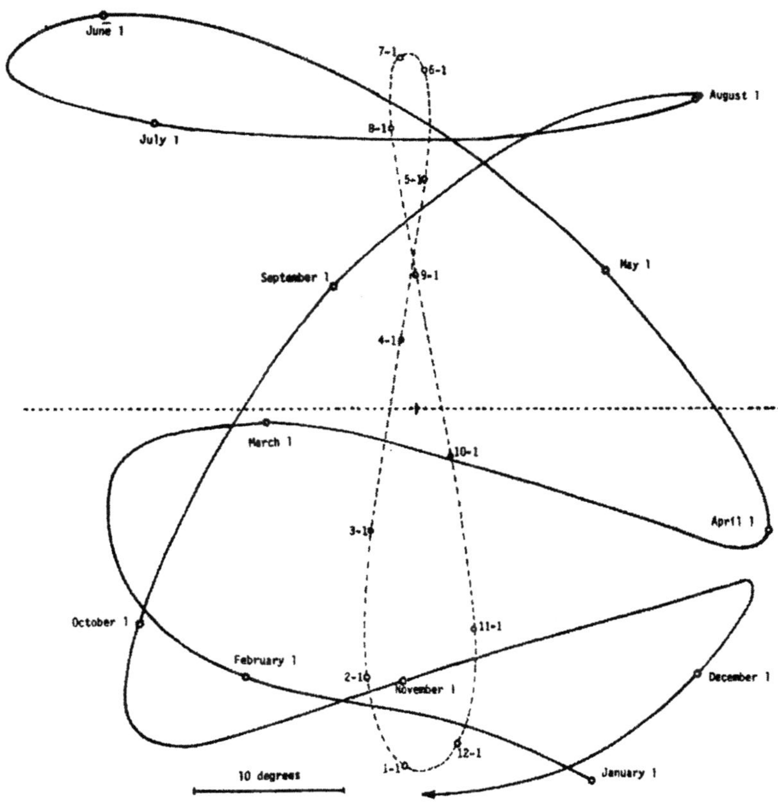

Figure 21. The curve of Mercury shown here for 1980, has both similarities and differences compared with that of 1979 (See Figure 20).

Figure 21 shows the corresponding but considerably different curve of Mercury for the following year, 1980. Here again the horizontal line indicates the celestial equator; the "figure 8" line, a joining together of the mean noon positions of the sun throughout the year. The curve of Mercury again starts low in winter, then lifts to summer heights, and finally descends once more in the following winter.

A comparison of the Mercury curve for 1979 (Figure 20) with that for 1980 (Figure 21) shows some elements of similarity and reflects in other respects considerable change. The loop in the upper left, for instance, has shrunk in 1980 as contrasted with 1979, but the loop in the upper right has slightly expanded. Also, the loop in the middle left, which reached up in 1979 drops down in 1980. Every curve is an individual event.

Figure 22 shows another picture of the Mercury curve of 1980, this time in a three-dimensional aspect. It is identical with the curve shown in Figure 21, but omitting all references to months, times and positions of the sun. The broken lines in Figure 22 indicate the portions of its path where Mercury is seen to light up most and shine; the solid lines, those portions where it fades more from view, loses visibility. Mercury comes nearer to us in the solid lines; is farther away in the broken lines. [Unlike Venus, Mercury shines brightest when it moves eastward on a curve which passes beyond the sun, in relation to the earth, and is in its gibbous to full phase. Ed.]

The Mercury curve is seen to change from year to year. Such pictures of planetary appearances suggest the remarkable flexibility of cosmic events, and help to make this cosmic flexibility manifest.

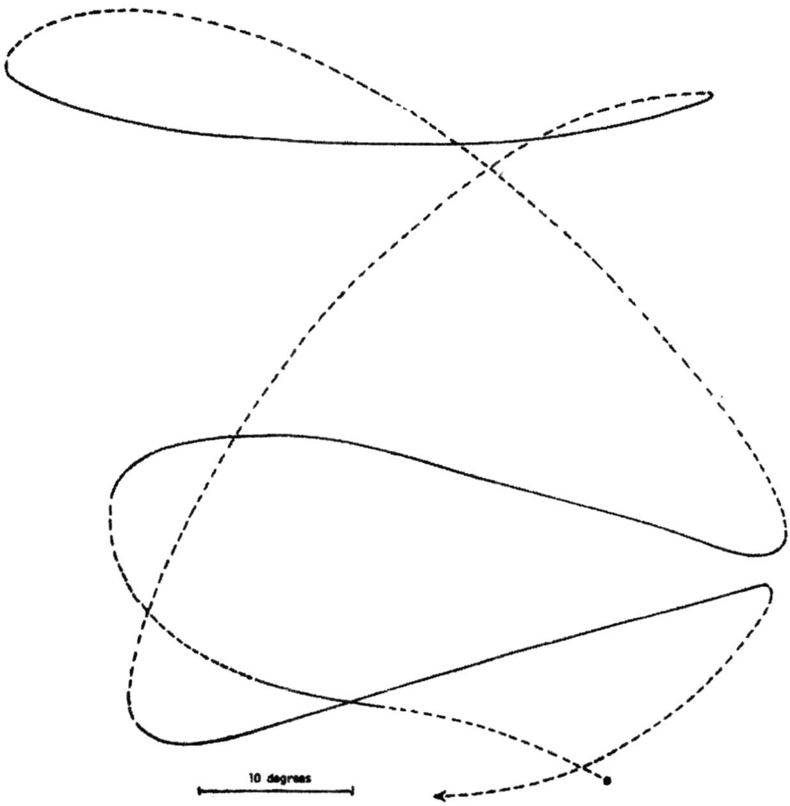

Figure 22. Three-dimensional aspect of Mercury's curve in 1980, with broken lines indicating portions of its path in which Mercury lights up and shines brightly, as seen from earth, and solid lines indicating portions where it shines less brightly.

VIII Observing the Zodiac

There are twelve star groups which are distinguished from the others, because they form most of the background against which the positions of the sun, moon and planets are seen for human observation. They comprise what is called the "zodiac." Figure 23 shows the twelve zodiacal constellations.

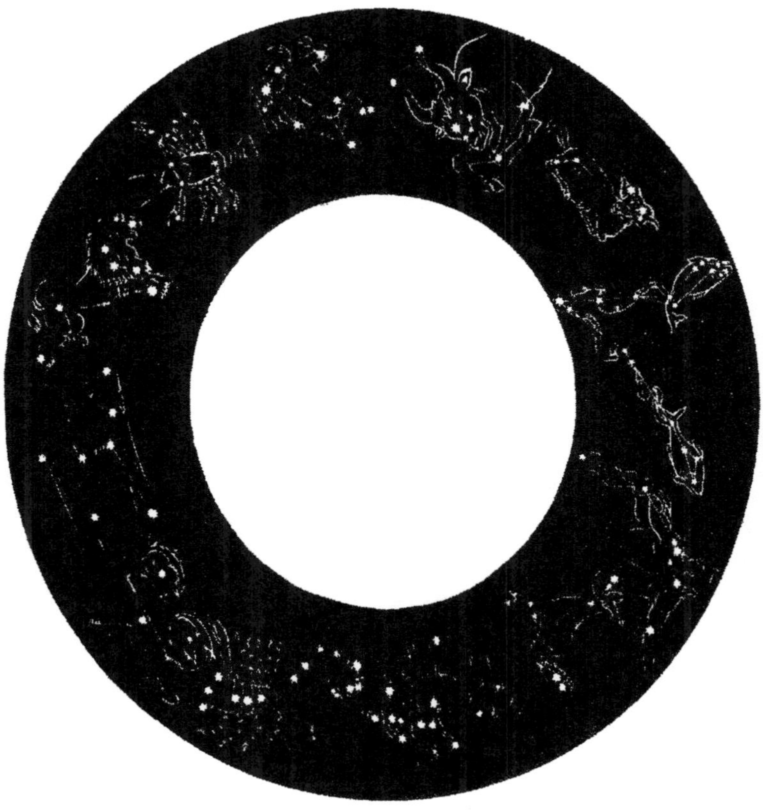

Figure 23. The zodiac's twelve star groupings, or constellations.

At the top of the circle in this picture are the constellations Taurus and Gemini, and to their immediate left, Cancer. Thence around the circle counterclockwise appear the twelve zodiacal star groups in the order in which the sun passes through them in one year, and which are listed below:

Taurus

Gemini

Cancer

Leo

Virgo

Libra

Scorpius

Sagittarius

Capricornus

Aquarius

Pisces

Aries

Among the stars on a clear night, half of the zodiac is always visible. From the position of the sun in relation to that of the moon or any planet, it is always possible to locate the zodiac. A semicircle connecting the position of the sun (as judged, for instance, by the center of the afterglow on the western horizon) with the moon or a planet, then continued from horizon to horizon across the whole sky, will pass through the zodiacal star groups.

Two of these twelve groups, Pisces and Virgo, lie opposite each other where the zodiacal circle crosses the celestial equator. They rise at the celestial equator in the east, and set at it in the west. They never leave it. The zodiacal star groups of Aries, Taurus, Gemini, Cancer and Leo essentially run their daily courses above the celestial equator; those of Libra, Scorpius, Sagittarius, Capricornus and Aquarius below it.

The highest of the daily courses above the celestial equator among these twelve star groups are the paths of Taurus and Gemini; the lowest, that of Sagittarius. When Gemini and Taurus stand high in the southern sky, they are near to the zenith. At such a time, the zodiac spans the sky from the east high over the south and down to the west. The zodiac rides in its highest position. [When the sun is at this highest position in the zodiac (at midsummer) it is in the astronomer's officially-designated constellation of Taurus, just beside the border with Gemini. This June solstice point of the sun moved over from Gemini to Taurus in 1989 as a result of the gradual movement (precession) of the equinoxes from east to west over thousands of years. Ed.]

Harmonic Movements of the Zodiac

When Sagittarius stands at its high point in the southern sky, it is low above the horizon as compared with the other constellations of the zodiac. At such a time, the zodiac is in its lowest position. Once in every twenty-four-hour period the zodiac appears in its high position, and once twelve hours later in its low position.

Throughout the course of the year, the zodiac's high and low positions come at different hours. In December, the high position comes at midnight; in June, the high position comes at midday; in December the low position comes at midday; in June the low position comes at midnight. All the lifting and lowering movements of the zodiac proceed in harmonic motion, spreading a truly beautiful rhythm around us.

In daytime, when we do not see the stars, the zodiac still rides above us. It is always there, though by day we do not see it because of the brightness of the sun. The sun moves through the zodiacal constellations in the course of a year—therefore, at noon in summer, when the zodiac stands in its high position, the star group Gemini/Taurus is concealed behind the sun. At noon in winter, when the zodiac stands in its low position, essentially the star group of Sagittarius is behind the sun.

In March and in September, when the sun is exactly on the celestial equator, it is in Pisces and Virgo respectively. Therefore the star group Pisces/Aquarius is invisible in March because the sun then shines within it. Because the stars move ahead of the sun in their daily course, each month another constellation rides through the sky with the sun. Times of the year when the sun can, in general, be found in particular zodiacal constellations, are as follows:

March/April	Pisces
April/May	Aries
May/June	Taurus
June/July	Gemini
July/August	Cancer
August/September	Leo
September/October	Virgo
(October)/November	Libra
November/(December)	Scorpius
December/January	Sagittarius
January/February	Capricornus
February/March	Aquarius

[Note: "December" in relation to Scorpius above, is in brackets because, although during December the sun passes above the tail of the Scorpion, it is nevertheless in the non-zodiacal constellation of

Ophiuchus. Also, the times of year when the sun is in particular constellations changes over long periods (see references to the precession of the equinoxes in the next section). For example, at the moment the sun is reckoned usually to enter the astronomer's conventional, star-map constellation of Libra just at the end of October (also in brackets above), but around the year 2047 it will establish itself in the constellation of Libra at the beginning of November. Ed.]

The Seasonal Year and the Precession of the Equinoxes

Over thousands of years, the constellations of the zodiac seem to gradually move eastwards in relation to the sun's seasonal positions in the sky. Put another way, the spring point of the sun slowly moves westwards and backwards through the constellations (to the right) so that at one period of history spring took place when the sun was in Taurus, and at a later period spring took place when the sun was in Aries.

Thus, at the time of the Greek and Latin civilizations, Aries rode with the sun around every March 21 (by our modern calendar), marking the start of spring. Aries was at the spring position of the sun and together with it on the celestial equator.

In still earlier times, Taurus occupied the spring position of the sun. The zodiac was at that time two constellations removed from the yearly positions of today in relation to the sun. If one now considers the constellations to be equal in length to each other, the time that passes before one constellation is replaced by the next in its relation to the sun is 2,150 years. Twice this number, 4,300 years backward in time, the ancient Egyptian era was in flower.

Not only the constellations of the zodiac, but all stars change in their relation to the sun. The position of the Pole Star was formerly occupied by other stars thousands of years ago. The rhythm of these changes for the whole zodiac is twelve times 2,150 years, or 25,800 years, sometimes called the "cosmic year". In 25,800 years from now, the sun will be riding again in the same zodiacal constellation in which it rides today at the spring of the year.

[It should be added that 25,800 years for a complete "precessional" cycle of the equinoxes is a generally accepted figure, though an attempt to be more accurate would arrive at 25,770 years. The figure of 25,920 years, sometimes referred to, is the result of rounding off the numbers, putting the sun's precessional movement at 1 degree in 72 years. Astronomically, the sun precesses 1 degree in about 71.6 years. Ed.]

Nothing in our universe is stationary. Everything is in a flow of motion and change, as Heraclitus noticed 2,500 years ago.

Closing Remarks

Would anyone consider the material contained in these chapters too complicated to be called an "Introduction to Astronomy"? Certainly young people have received it in the past with interest and enthusiasm. Even many who are far from being botanists study the forms of flowers and leaves, which are scarcely too complicated for the understanding despite their intricacy and richness. Why should a study of the stars seem more forbidding?

For human beings, old and young, the direct language of ordinary observation creates a fresh, lively attitude toward the cosmos, such as no kind of human-made interpretation or deduction can possibly produce, despite descriptions of all manner of celestial explosions, dazzling speeds, cosmic collisions, etc.

The stars will reveal their secrets, the secrets of the universe, to the person who looks inquiringly and humanly upon them. An understanding of what the stars convey about themselves can help the observer to correspondingly develop an attitude toward the whole of life which opens other people to these cosmic truths and renders the facts contained in them more comprehensible and of greater value.

It is so great what the stars can tell humanity of orderly movement and harmony. It is so great what human beings can tell one another of the deepest and most impressive truths of human life in a universe of such grandeur as the stars demonstrate it to be.